COWMAN

Church of the Holy Sunrise, Vol. II

A story of life on the South Dakota prairie in free verse
by award-winning poet and rancher,

Bruce Roseland

Copyright © Bruce Roseland, 2018. No part of this book may be reproduced or distributed in any form or by any means, or stored in a data base or retrieval system, without written permission from the author. All rights, including electronic, are reserved by the author.

Printed in the United States of America.

First edition 2018.

Cover photograph by Adam Roseland.

Scurfpea Publishing
P.O. Box 46
Sioux Falls, SD 57101
scurfpeapublishing.com
editor@scurfpeapublishing.com

Contents

Introduction
Our daily grit   1
    Pasque Petals, published by SD State Poetry Society, Fall 2014
The truth is   2
O.K. to cry   3
    Pasque Petals, published by SD State Poetry Society, Fall 2014
One day at a time   4
My days of future past   6
My early childhood education   7
    Pasque Petals, published by SD State Poetry Society, Spring 2013
When Google doesn't work   8
My town   9
What this land is made of   10
    Pasque Petals, published by SD State Poetry Society, Fall 2015
Each day we send them off   11
Proof of life   12
    Pasque Petals, published by SD State Poetry Society, Spring 2017
Afternoon date   13
The only beauty shop in town   14
The view from the back of the room   15
    The Cattle Business Weekly, Phillip, SD, 2015
2 Americas   16
Good rodeo   18
Tinder dry   20

Job description   21
Jim's tire repair   22
I dream of disasters   24
The starting-out years   25
Last visit   26
The old rancher meditation   27
    Pasque Petals, published by SD State Poetry Society, Fall 2015
One of the tough ones   28
Broke   30
    Pasque Petals, published by SD State Poetry Society, Fall 2016
Point of view   31
Neighborhood watch   32
Recognition   33
End of the day   34
The lay of the land   35
Strong ties   36
Landscape only I see   37
Apples   38
    Pasque Petals, published by SD State Poetry Society, Spring 2012
Winter from hell 1996-97   40
Flight or fight   41
Bad day at the ranch   42
Unscheduled vacation   43
Repair   44
Rites of life   45
Near miss   46
Next time   47
Farmer laureate at 63   48
    The Scandalous Lives of Butterflies, edited by Kevin Cole,
      Scurfpea Publishing, Sioux Falls, SD, 2015
Ritual   49
Duct tape   50
Facts of life for a native   51
Waiting   52
Not enough grass   53

There is magic in the ability to take 26 little letters of the alphabet and assemble them into words that describe life, both past and present, on the harsh plains of the Dakotas. Bruce Roseland is a magician who has lived that life and describes it through his artistic and emotional poetry. *COWMAN* will remain for future generations to explore the lifestyle of a cattleman as well as our American heritage.
— Yvonne Hollenbeck,
Cowboy Poet & Rancher

COWMAN has the feel of a novel or a memoir, continuing day to day and season to season. The poet/cowman is altogether authentic and believable — terse, straight-forward, tough in mind and body, empathetic, neighborly, curious, optimistic, philosophical. The land he works on and owns is "made out of/cattle, steel, and wheat,/tires gripping the road,/thunderheads piled high in the sky,/blizzards howling in the night,/seasons green, seasons white,/muscle and bone, grit and sweat/on the arms of working stiffs." This matter-of-fact cowman describes the details of calving, and dealing with protective mothers that have given him serious injuries. He celebrates the powerful life force in a new-born calf, "From the first gasp of air/into the newborn's lungs . . . ." In one poem he visits an old neighbor: "There you were, good neighbor, good friend,/after a lifetime of work/your body stiffened by pain,/a mind grown quiet,/sitting with a bib around your neck,/being spoon fed." He has a strong sense of history, including his own family's, saying of his grandfather: "He stuck his stake in the virgin soil,/built his soddie, and sent for his bride." He knows nature can be merciless: in "Montana is Burning" he looks at the smoke covering the countryside, ending the poem with, "I am breathing the death of a million trees." He is keenly observant of and shows great empathy for creatures; dragonflies, for instance, "on the top wire of a barbed-wire fence/in 90-degree, windless heat . . . clinging to the razor-sharp tips of the barbs," as he's working on the fence. In another poem, he sees an owl "hunting the scratchy trails/ of mice racing across icy snow." The book is full of close, meticulous, at times philosophical observations. In "Moonshine," the cowman's yard is so lit up by the moon at night that he can read a newspaper: "When was it that we became afraid/of the dark, like death, hiding in our cities of light?" He ends the poem by imagining (and admonishing the reader): "walking out, striding over the land,/disappearing into the shadows to find/the mystery that you know has/always been on the very edge of your life./Find a road./Follow the moonshine." In the end, this cowman's life is hard but finally worthwhile: "You'll find me where light meets darkness,/where earth touches sky . . . with early morning sunshine/full upon my thankful face." With *COWMAN*, Bruce Roseland becomes one of a number of fine poets with books about farm and ranch life on the American plains: James Hearst, Leo Dangel, Bill Kloefkorn, and Linda Hasselstrom come to mind. Good company, for sure. And well-deserved.

– David Allen Evans,
South Dakota Poet Laureate

Mirage   54
Snow and rain make grass   55
    Pasque Petals, published by SD State Poetry Society, Fall 2012
Drought of '17   56
    The Cattle Business Weekly, Phillip, SD, 6/21/17
Absentee owner   57
Montana is burning/September 13, 2017   58
    The Cattle Business Weekly, Phillip, SD, 9/27/17
Defiance   59
Getting ahead of the forecast   60
Night moves   61
    The Cattle Business Weekly, Phillip, SD, 4/16
The primeval heart   62
First calf   64
Calving season   66
The will to survive   67
Easter morning 2015   68
Hidden in plain sight   69
    Thunderstorm, edited by Steve Boint,
    Scurfpea Publishing, Sioux Falls, SD, 2013
Slap!   70
    Pasque Petals, published by SD State Poetry Society, Spring 2012
    and *Thunderstorm*, edited by Steve Boint,
    Scurfpea Publishing, Sioux Falls, SD, 2013
Last calf   71
Compulsion   72
The gift bearer   74
None of my business   75
Bull-headed   76
Day's end   77
The drawback   78
    Pasque Petals, published by SD State Poetry Society, Spring 2012
Work buddies   79
The haymaker's dance   80
The best-laid web   81

The other side   82
Man vs plants   83
August/cow country   84
Good day's work   85
Inheritance   86
Late October   87
Weed seed celebration   88
    Thunderstorm, edited by Steve Boint,
    Scurfpea Publishing, Sious Falls, SD, 2013
Miserable (or a state of mind)   89
The promise   90
    Pasque Petals, published by SD State Poetry Society, Fall 2011
Fall weaning   91
    Pasque Petals, published by SD State Poetry Society, Fall 2013
Cull cows   92
Poet as full-time cowman   93
    Pasque Petals, published by SD State Poetry Society, Fall 2012
Gimme shelter   94
Eden retold   95
Fattening up   96
    I Walked by the River, edited by Brandyn Johnson,
    Scurfpea Publishing, Sioux Falls, SD, 2016
The belly of a cow   97
Buy a cow and save the planet   98
Moonshine   99
    Pasque Petals, published by SD State Poetry Society, Fall 2010
Rock of ages   100
Real estate open house   102
Ablution   103
    Pasque Petals, published by SD State Poetry Society, Fall 2016
All is not over   104
Mates   105
Night hunter   106
    Pasque Petals, published by SD State Poetry Society, Fall 2013

His meal   107
Momma cat   108
Taking a walk on the wild side   109
Sanctuary   110
> *Pasque Petals*, published by SD State Poetry Society, Spring 2013

Night begins   112
> *I Walked by the River*, edited by Brandyn Johnson,
> Scurfpea Publishing, Sioux Falls, SD, 2016

Return of the native   113
Good earth   114
> *Pasque Petals*, published by SD State Poetry Society, Spring 2013
> and *Thunderstorm*, edited by Steve Boint,
> Scurfpea Publishing, Sioux Falls, SD, 2013

Net worth   115
> *Pasque Petals*, published by SD State Poetry Society, Spring 2012
> and *Thunderstorm*, edited by Steve Boint,
> Scurfpea Publishing, Sioux Falls, SD, 2013

Hot-tubbing on New Year's Eve   116
A year turns   117
> *Pasque Petals*, published by SD State Poetry Society, Spring 2013
> and *Thunderstorm*, edited by Steve Boint,
> Scurfpea Publishing, Sioux Falls, SD, 2013

Where the heart is   118
A regular   119
> *Church of the Holy Sunrise*, written by Bruce Roseland
> with photographs by Susan Melius, self-published, 2012

About the author   121

This book is dedicated to Barb.

Introduction

In the open wide
of prairie
what we have is what you see.

Our daily grit

Many of us roll a rock
that only we know
up the same mountain each day.
The next morning we find
that very same rock
has rolled back into the valley
from which it came.
Again and again we set our shoulder
to this rock
with our sights on the mountain,
and heave.

For all those who each day get up and give 'er all they got.

The truth is

If your living depends
on the land you tend
day after day
through one year
and the next year
into a lifetime
of both good
and bad,
this occupation can deliver
into your hands and upon your body
the shape of the man you've become,
whether you meant
for this to happen
or not.
The words you speak friend to friend,
neighbor to neighbor,
carry the weight of this life,
show the spirit that lies within.
This land, your land,
has hewed your body,
leaving the edges to harden.
This is the you
that steps out to greet each new day,
seeing tomorrow
just over the prairie's rim.

O.K. to cry

Written after the sudden death of my wife, Barb. We were married 34 and a half years.

The funeral was just a thing
to endure,
a ritual
wrapped in coffee and cakes,
prayers the living repeat
to make sense of the senseless.
But when I looked into the mourners eyes,
when my hands clasp
their hands,
30 years as their everyday neighbor,
30 years as their everyday friend,
I see they actually care.
My pain is their pain;
their pain is my pain.
Two and half weeks have gone by
and I'm knocking around this house.
The sounds
are not the sounds of quiet
but of empty.

I see you leaving as a golden astral ray
like sunrise, like sunset,
going the distance,
starting out at my eye level,
going, gone over the blue horizon.

One day at a time

A lengthy snowstorm had finally quieted
after piling snow up higher than our windows,
shuddering our wood-framed,
one-story house with gusty blows.
My father and his brother's small "M" tractor
could not break through the heavy drifts
to feed their cattle.
This was the 1950's, when engines
had replaced horses.
But my dad and uncle, like many others,
hadn't the heart to sell the horses.
With cow ponies, they rode out
to find the heavy draft work horses
which had drifted away with the storm.
I had my mother stuff me into heavy, cold-weather gear
so I could go out and play
in the white wonderland.
Standing atop a snowdrift, I watched
my dad and uncle drive the big-limbed
draft animals past me.

The thick-haired animals' powerful hooves
cleaved the deep banks of snow,
spraying powdery plumes
as they ploughed through one drift
and then plunged through another,
making their way to the barn
and waiting harnesses.
Snow glittered all around them
in the bright, crystal-cold sunshine.
They would spend the next days and weeks
pulling sleds of hay to hungry cattle,
hay that had been hand-pitched
from snowed-over haystacks,
back-breaking work in miserably cold weather.
Standing in Dakota air
watching those magnificent animals,
I was unaware of how young I was,
unaware that I was a witness to
the remnants of a certain past,
my own future yet to unfold.

My days of future past

I heard the voices of tomorrow
calling on an autumn day,
when a birthday cake with candles
my mother had made
was waiting for me.
She asked how old was I,
and I laughed and said "five."
From the wavering prairie grass
I was playing in,
wind blew whispers
of what was to come;
gone as soon as I listened.
Still I knew even then
I would hear those voices again
somewhere in a future day,
and I would follow.

My early childhood education

In early-spring snowstorms, my father
would come in from the outside
and dump a nearly lifeless,
snow-encrusted newborn calf
on the linoleum floor of the living room
in front of our oil-fed furnace.
He would then walk back out to
deal with other troubles.
I wasn't yet old enough to be useful outdoors;
instead, I kept an eye on the calf, watching
him shiver uncontrollably with the ice melting
off his body in puddles
that were mopped up by my mother.
Slowly, the calf would warm,
lift up his head,
and tuck his legs under his body,
deciding to live.
This I watched and studied,
seeing the near-dead return
to the living.
My father would smile
when he came back into the house
to see me holding down a wobbly baby calf
trying to scrabble around on a slick floor.
He would lift and cradle the calf
in his over-coated arms
and carry it back to its rightful mother,
a victory in the often hard-fought battles
of early-spring blizzards.

When Google doesn't work

Long-lost girlfriends, boyfriends, old friends
can be found in South Dakota by motoring
to their old hometown, stepping through
the front door of the local café,
taking a seat at the lunch counter, and
asking the oldest waitress,
"Did you ever know so-and-so
and where they went?"
And, as long as your clothes are clean
and there is no strangeness in your eye,
you'll get your answer,
IF you wait until after
talking about the weather,
having a cup of coffee,
and ordering some apple pie.

My town

Hometown is when,
walking down the sidewalk
next to a busy highway
running through the sleepy downtown,
half the drivers in the cars
wave.
Some out of curiosity of what you're up to,
the rest because there is business
with you needing doing.

What this land is made of

This land is made out of
cattle, steel, and wheat,
tires gripping the road,
thunderheads piled high in the sky,
blizzards howling in the night,
seasons green, seasons white,
muscle and bone, grit and sweat
on the arms of working stiffs.
Young men grow,
making their dreams.
That's what this country is made of.
Books and brains, domain names,
google and twitter fact checked,
G.P.S. high tech connected,
internetted.
Everything, everyone at your finger-tip's
click.
Dow goes up; jobs go down.
One foot in, one foot out.
Swing for the fence;
bases are covered
until they are not.
Lightning strikes on a clear blue day.
Everything looks random
until you look back.

Each day we send them off

On an early morning, in the early fall
I am rolling down a back road
pulling a stock trailer
when one of my neighbor's old cars,
his kid alone at the wheel,
zips around and by me
doing 80 or better.
Soon the passing car careens to the right,
touching the road shoulder, puffing up
gravel dust, then corrects back
to the road's center line.
An error of judgment, no doubt,
either while dialing up the CD's volume
or, more likely yet,
texting his high school buddies –
sharing the latest overnight
hot teenage gossip
while they too drive on in to school
from the other far corners of the county.
In the back window of the receding car,
written in crayola grease paint:
PLAY NICE ! GO WIN ! # 77

Proof of life

In the '70's, we local youths
climbed an iron-rung ladder
up the cement-sided grain elevator
of our small upper-midwestern town.
In the near-shadowy darkness,
lit as much by stars and moon
as by the town's illuminations,
we reached a flat, guardrail-less rooftop.
There we would sit back from the edge in silence,
daring not to talk
since voices would travel far
in the clear windless night air of a town
whose citizens were in bed after the 10 o'clock news.
The town's cop was keeping his usual lonesome watch
down by the gas station,
sitting in his car, engine off, windows
rolled down, police radio squawking.
From the elevator's rooftop the view was magnificent;
above, the universe blazed mystical,
below, streetlights ran crisscross,
checkerboarded to the very edge
where town met farmland.
Out on the blue, black horizon,
night sky met earth, broken only
by isolated pin pricks of solitary farm yard lights.
Way further off, glowed towns miles and miles away
where other souls,
other lives, Homo Sapiens Sapiens, had to be,
just had to be, stirring, moving toward something greater.

Afternoon date

The woman was stick-thin, old,
scuffling slow, seeking the booth
next to mine in Perkins.
Halfway across the restaurant,
she adjusted her piled-up white hair
and the whole works shifted.
Of course, a wig.
Behind her came her man.
Elderly, but still moving well,
his eyes only on her,
his arm reached for her elbow
until his sight landed on me.
"Bruce?" he said, "Bruce?"
And that's when I realized
that I, a far long ways from home,
have happened upon old neighbors
who, upon retiring, had moved away.
As they settled into their booth,
and I with them,
we talked about the old days,
crops and the chance of rain.
I sipped my coffee
as their meals were brought in.
I watch him eat his full plate
as he watched her eat
half a sandwich of grilled cheese,
encouraging the bites with his eyes
because each bite bought her a little more time.
Their Saturday afternoon routine.
A few months later
I read in the paper she had died.

The only beauty shop in town

An empty box of Menthol Marlboro Lights
lay uncrushed
next to a flattened hawk,
his black and white wings outstretched
against the asphalt,
just recently peeled off
the silver grill of a red 4x4 pickup truck
parked curbside
by one of the regulars
on her way to her weekly
wash and set.

The view from the back of the room

In the last sundown rosy light of a cold January day,
I made my way to Dick Edgar's wake.
The warmth of the car heater felt good
as I traveled past the quiet, rolling native
pastures and cropland of central South Dakota.
Upon arriving at the funeral home, I found one
of the last remaining seats at the back of the room.
There I listened to the prayers and tributes
to this gentleman cowman as he was sent off to his last reward.
Dick was always part of the outfit that carried his name;
the backbone, the quiet brains,
the one that made his family a family.
Every man who drove into his yard to buy a bull –
if they weren't already a neighbor – left as one.
So there in the back of the room, I got to thinking,
not just of him – but of us gathered in that room.
Seat after seat of men and women in front of me
solid as the land is solid.
The younger and older generations intermingled;
sitting together, having the look of those who spend
a lot of time working outdoors and liking what they do,
the look of the fit and contented.
Some folks may think of their eventual retirement,
but many that I know who work with cows, don't.
There's always another calf crop on the way;
another hay crop to bring in
until the good Lord comes calling.
For Dick Edgar, it was 88 years,
for the rest of us, we hope to do as well.
If you want to see the harvest of a person's life,
his times, family, the good neighbors –
sit in back of the room.
The view is powerful.

2 Americas

Spring of '14
at Sioux Falls "U,"
I watched my one and only nephew
get hooded and join
the rank of MD's.
Young, bright, a serious lot
relieved to be finally on the stage
cheered on by an auditorium 1,000 strong –
relatives, friends, supporters.
Later a reception at the Starlight Room,
Downtown Holiday Inn.
I had reserved a room, staying overnight.
Woke up at first light
and couldn't find a thing open downstairs
at 6:30 AM serving coffee and eggs.
I walked halfway down Phillips Ave,
rattled the door at the silver diner café.
Not open yet either.
Saw just one man
on the empty sidewalks,

walking his morning jog,
eyes down and straight ahead,
nervously said "Hi,"
as I boomed out "Hello!"
Not a car was on the streets,
just a garbage truck rolling
through a yellow light.
While out on the outskirts
and all across the small towns,
the convenience store coffee shops
have been open since before 6
with guys in their work gear organizing their days,
buying straight black coffee and chips,
then heading out on service calls,
retirees lining the side-booths,
working on their 2nd cup,
waiting for today's news to walk in.
Back at the hotel, I laid
the key card on the main desk,
pulled out of the nearly-full parking garage
and joined the Interstate traffic west.

Good rodeo

On a Sunday afternoon with the sun at his back,
halfway between the chutes and the boxes,
Harold, fully relaxed, leaned
against the fence of the rodeo arena,
his hat tilted up and a big ol' grin on his face.
He was watching his grandson
barreling out on a fast horse to race a red, long-legged steer
flank to flank, then neck to neck,
sliding off to grip the steer's horns
and twist with all his youthful power
until the steer ploughed into the ground
amid a haze of dust, a union of man, beast, and earth.
With a whump of a hand, his grandson
brushed the dirt off his clothes as both
he and the steer walked away,
neither much the worse for wear.

Many years later, I was there when Harold was laid to rest
on another sunny, blue-sky day.
He had been a big, tall man
who reminded me of one of those great
cottonwood trees that stands
on the edge of a prairie slough, a landmark that we rely on
to get our directions straight, sorely missed
after a raging storm finally brings it down.

He was carried to his grave
in a Studebaker triple-box wagon
with the top two planks taken off,
pulled by a roan Belgian team,
living stand-ins for Bert and Ernie,
the black Percheron team
that had rehabilitated him
from a stroke several years previous to this.
The Belgian team was driven by his two sons
and following were his grandsons on horseback,
riding escort to a heart-shaped headstone
engraved with the words, "faith", "hope", "love."
At the cemetery, his family and friends filed past,
each placing single-stemmed Black-eyed Susans,
a reminder of the native prairie he so loved,
atop the casket
as their final good-bye to him,
bidding farewell to a man
who had never felt that life contained so little,
or was too short,
but rather understood
that we all have so much
if we just look.

Tinder dry

A puff of haze hangs over the neighbor's trees
two country miles away.
"Must be the hay grinder starting up,"
but the grey turns to black
puffs of smoke. "Holy mackerel!"
I say to myself and head down the road
toward a climbing, billowing column
that only fire can produce.
I pull up into my neighbor's yard.
There, in a clear square of grass
between buildings and hay bales
stands his loader tractor,
diesel fuel tank on fire,
flames leaping ten feet into the air.
The cab, now windowless,
drips molding down in flaming little gobs.
My neighbor, standing 30 feet
upwind from the tractor
is squirting a garden hose on the
still surviving tires,
trying to keep them cool.
A small crowd of hired men, family,
and the curious that have stopped
off the road stand back, watching silently.
"The Fire Department is on its way," I'm told.
I catch my neighbor's eye and shout to him,
"You don't have to start a fire to get me
to drop by."
He nods and smiles a bit grimly
as he continues to lay a steady stream
on the lit-up, gutted-out,
100,000-dollar-plus tractor.
There's nothing here for me to do
except go back to my own workday.

Job description

Overcast skies frequently spit snow
and intermittent freezing rain –
no place for a calf
to be born this April of 2011.
Snow fell each night and part of each day
in the cattle yards, turning the muck white
as cows' hooves churned
and punched ever deeper,
leaving pockmarks of water and ice –
calves birthed
into this slop,
chilling them so badly that they could not get up
to find their mothers and nurse.
A cousin told me that his daughter had asked him,
"When does this let up, Dad? When is this done?"
after two-plus solid weeks of night-and-day
dragging calves into the barn to dry off,
pairing them with their frequently cantankerous mothers
to get started nursing as quickly as possible
and then, kicking them back out into the weather
to fend on their own
in order to make room
to shelter the even more newly-born.
Looking out on a landscape
that appeared more winter than spring,
he had told her, "When it's done,"
and took the next step
to get the next newborn calf
out of the water, rain, snow, and mud.

Jim's tire repair

When a rear tire on one of my tractors goes flat,
I call up Jim, a big man.
"What size is it?" he always asks.
"Damn," I say, "I'll have to check –
I'll call you back."
And when I do, he comes right to my place;
Sundays, sunshine, or storm, he arrives
to air-jack the heavy axles off the ground,
pry the rubber off the rim with splayed irons,
and wrestle these huge tires that are
taller than my head.
He manhandles them back onto their rims,
all in good humor, cussing his way through the work.
He's been a tire man for years,
proud of the work he does.
When the work is done, I pay him.
Then we talk.
Today, he talks about his black Lab
that travels everywhere with him.
"This dog has me trained," he says.
"Before I can work on a tire,
I have to lay out fresh dog food
and a pan with water.

Only then does he let me go to work."
Summertimes, Jim will stop
next to deep sloughs and throw
softball-sized rocks into the water.
The dog leaps in, diving into two feet of water,
retrieves the rock,
drops it at Jim's feet,
and then they repeat.
With a big grin, Jim says he regrets
he didn't meet the dog before
he'd met his ex-wife.
He hands me a couple of pocket-size calendars
featuring bare-breasted ladies,
a different one for each month.
He hands them out every year
to all his customers.
He says it's a Christmas gift,
even though it's now mid-March.
Then, on second thought,
he hands me a Chippendale calendar
with twelve different bare-breasted men
on it.
"This one's for your wife."

I dream of disasters

I dream of disasters in my sleep,
terrible things that have no end,
choices that turn around and around
to grab their own tails,
dogs of dreams,
events that are intense,
blizzards that do not end,
of snow piling up,
of calves being born
with no safe place to put them,
with more calves being born
and no place to put them.
Snow piles up with
losses I cannot stop.
On waking,
the dark comforts me not.
Why am I in bed?
Isn't a blizzard raging?
Then I realize it is not
the season for calving.
It is not the right month
and a different year
than when I last woke up to hear
the sounds of disaster raging.
My nightmares are re-enactments
of battles too real,
tricks of the nighttime mind.

The starting-out years

A thin young man
in short-sleeved shirt, leaning forward, gripped
the steering wheel of a 1950-some International tractor
which was trailing a double Rowse mower
engulfed in a cloud of gravel dust.
He gave a quick wave in passing;
his attention was focused on the pebbly road.
I knew a little of his story –
working his way into his grandfather's place.
The sun was on the edge of setting.
Behind him, a beat-up pickup followed,
lights flashing, wanting to be sure of being seen.
Inside the cab was a lean young woman
hunched over the steering wheel, hair cut short,
eyes intent on following the dust up ahead,
husband and wife moving equipment around.
No doubt, they'll be up again early tomorrow,
racing the day to dark.

Last visit

There you were,
good neighbor, good friend,
after a lifetime of work
your body stiffened by pain,
a mind grown quiet,
sitting with a bib around your neck
being spoon fed.
The nursing home staff had you
fresh shaved pink and bathed and hair combed neat.
You and I had always had something
to say every time we would meet.
Today the talk beyond my hello
never began.
I knew your attendant, a high school
classmate of mine,
and while you methodically ate breakfast,
she and I reminisced about old times,
our class reunion coming up,
and small talk about those we knew.
When time began its dragging feeling,
I rose from my chair saying goodbye,
then I heard you clear as a bell
say, "Thanks for dropping by."
Startled, I said, "See you again."
But within a month you died.

The old rancher meditation

My body aches
in just about every place
where muscle meets bone.
One year it's my right shoulder,
the next year, my left.
Where the bursitis burst
and the tendons tear
from the unexpected yanks,
ramps up the daily wear
to sorely impaired.
I must bow my head
to comb my hair.
What hair that is left there.
When I complain
to my companions of work
they only laugh, "Pain is good,"
they say. "Lets you know
you are still alive."
For those who have grown old
in this profession of mine,
all abhor being useless and bored.
To die in their stride
is their wish.
The good Lord willing,
this we shall each get.

One of the tough ones

"He was hard on machinery,
hard on women, hard on himself,"
said his brother about Frank.
To this he, at least, partially agreed,
having been married three times.
His first died from cancer,
divorced his 2nd after a stormy marriage,
and managed to die while still married to his third.
I worked several years with Frank,
in my teenage years cutting corn for silage.
He ran the cutter and I drove
the wagons to the pile.
Some mornings he had the first loads
waiting in the yard at sunrise,
saying he might as well climb
onto the tractor and get started
since he could hear it yammering
in his head while lying in bed.
To keep up shuttling the wagons,
I kept the throttle wide open.
Around about 4 in the afternoon
he would dig a pint of whiskey
from the tool box and kill it all

in the less-than-a-minute
while we exchanged silage wagons.
Then we would keep cutting
to plumb, black dark –
a style of work I became accustomed to.
One May, the deer were eating his tomato plants.
In order to make an enclosure,
he drove steel posts into the ground,
cutting the propane line to his house.
The gas followed the break, filling his basement.
When he flipped the light switch,
the boom lifted his house
off the foundation a foot, according to the flashings
pushed upward on the chimney.
He had been standing in the open basement door.
Badly burnt, he went outside,
shutting off the propane tank.
Then he drove to his brother's house two miles away,
where his charred clothes were cut
from his body with scissors.
He lived three days before he died.
One of eight children,
most of whom lived to be over 90.
Frank made it to 69.

Broke

Grey of hair, his wife served
his solitary potato baked
in its skin on a simple dish
set on a wooden table that held two chairs,
one for him, one for me.
He mashed his potato with his fork,
placing a gob of margarine
in the forks' tracks, salted and peppered,
then methodically began to eat
as he told me the price
of the land he needed to sell.
His eyes and face were as flat
as his dining plate.

His eyes never left that potato.

Point of view

An older rancher driving down a county highway
late at night with his wife
sees tractor lights in a field,
remarks to her,
"There's a guy who's apparently
not getting along with his wife,"
and laughs.
She repeats to my wife
her husband's remark and says,
"If you ever see my husband's tractor lights
moving in a field late at night,
remember: his choice, not mine."

Neighborhood watch

I wondered who was visiting
with the help
as I pulled up with my trailer
to load the last of my cattle
from a dusty corral.
It was the fellow
who lived nearby
on a bit of land
on which he ran some horses –
his grandkids rode them
when they came out to visit
and played farmer-and-cowboy.
They were about the only ones
I would see on my weekly pasture checks.
I'd say hello to this bushy-bearded neighbor
when I'd be dropping off
or picking up my cattle
on this faraway rented land.
He would notice my trailing gravel dust
and come by to chat.
Maybe he was being just friendly,
or maybe something more,
wanting to know just who it was
in his neck of the prairie on any particular day.
I do know that in all my years
of running cattle
on this isolated pasture ground,
I have never lost a corral panel
or a cow or calf.
Some folks might call this luck,
but I'm not that dumb.
Luck is frequently
a pair of watching eyes.

Recognition

I pulled off the Interstate
far from home, in need of gas.
On my way to the counter inside
to pay for my fill-up,
a Western-dressed, tall and lanky,
white-haired man in a cowboy hat
said, "Hi, how are you?"
Surprised, I grunted an "OK" back.
I'd never seen him before.
In a crowded gas station,
I was the only one he greeted.
Strange about that – since I was wearing
nondescript bluejeans, a t-shirt, and no hat.
I heard a Buddhist saying once: "Your Karma
walks before you."
Perhaps, among cowmen, it's the cowman's life
that somehow one cowman recognizes
when he meets another, no matter
what garb he's wearing.

End of the day

Under a sky of darkest blue,
a half moon hangs
at 11 o'clock
as the big bale processor's
two-foot-long knives whirl
to a clanging halt.
Bill, the owner/operator, pries
the hay screen out of the tracks
of the hay grinders gaping maw
and heaves the 100-plus pounds
of iron sieve
over the side to clatter
on the frozen ground;
a job needing doing
before the January overnight temps
freeze the works into place.
400 bales totaling 300 tons,
a good day's work done.
Now, a twenty-four mile trip back home.
Up tomorrow again for a 12-hour grind,
if wind doesn't blow
and iron doesn't break.

The lay of the land

My hay-hauler hauls hay
for many different folks
in an area ranging a hundred miles or so
in all four directions from where he lives.
He lives about fifty miles from me.
I told him over the phone about a stack
I wanted hauled in from a field he'd never been to before,
giving him directions to where it sits,
a mile west of a neighbor who lives
seven miles from me down a graveled backstretch of road.
"Oh, yeah, I seen that stack sitting alone," he said,
"the other day while I was hauling for someone else."
Somewhere in the back of his mind, as his truck
lumbers along bearing the weight of 20-ton-plus loads,
his own internal GPS is always turned on.

Strong ties

From the east,
across the fresh cut
of black, Dakota Territory dirt,
steel rails were laid on oak ties.
Over these, the homesteaders carried
their possessions and dreams
into the vastness of prairie grass.
In the year 1886 the railroad, reaching
Redfield, SD, brought these settlers,
one of which was my great grandfather Gabe.
He stepped into the green promise of spring
and walked 50 miles due west
until something about the rolling land
struck his eye.
This, he felt, he could make home.
He stuck his stake in the virgin soil,
built his soddie, and sent for his bride.
Together they worked their fate out
through thick and thin.
Today, on nearly every quarter of land
I own that touches the original home place,
strong corner posts of railroad ties
anchor the fences
through which my family generations
of sweat and pride
claimed the right
to live under Dakota sky.

Landscape only I see

In the 1920's and 30's,
my grandfather moved deserted buildings
in from nearby abandoned homesteads.
Of these dreams gone bad,
he made hog houses and sheds.
After 50 years of rooting hogs,
gnawing rats, and just plain rot,
their usefulness dead-ended.
These were the buildings I tore down,
one at a time with sledge, saw and chain,
dragging sections of wood-shingled roofs,
2x6 lumbered sides, to a burning site,
where upon the black ashes
of previously burnt buildings,
I poured gasoline and tossed a torch,
making a bonfire out of wreck.
Sparks flew upward,
landing in nearby grass to burn haphazardly.
I, the guardian of the fire,
stepped upon the embers, putting them out.
Through my mind's eye, I still see
where they had stood –
ghosts
where sky and ground meet.

Apples

Lifeless, ice-encrusted black lumps
of baby calves lay where they dropped.
The half-light of sunrise revealed,
after the three-day blizzard of April 13, 1986,
barely-moving mother cows
shuffling through still-drifting snow,
going from dead calf to dead calf,
sniffing and lowing.
The cattle yard had been a war zone
of bad spring weather.
Several cows that had lost their calves
didn't give up,
mothering a few of the still-living calves
away from their original mothers.
I felt defeated, exhausted,
after fighting the blizzard
and then spending hard days
trying to straighten out the mess
that followed.
The drifts were so bad I had shoveled out

only an inclined path through a snowbank
blocking my house door.
Just after lunch a week after the storm,
I heard a thump against the door –
the mailman had slid down a wrapped package
of apple tree seedlings
which I had ordered a month before.
The week after they arrived,
I planted them in my muddy, flooded
backyard,
not sure, after such a disaster,
whether I'd be staying around
to see them grow.
Yet, in the Mays that followed,
I had pink apple blossoms fluttering
in the sunshine and wind, greeting me
whenever I emerged from the calving yards.
Now, in the fall 20-some years later,
I have red apples against October sky.

Winter from hell 1996-97

The snow came early;
by Thanksgiving the banks were already
four to five foot in the fence lines and trees.
In early December, blizzards came
regularly every few days.
As temps dropped, the snow would fall
from the blinding-white sky suddenly
until you couldn't see 100 feet ahead.
Motorists became lost and were rescued
from highways impassible for
thirty to fifty miles at a stretch.
Each day at my homestead, I dug out
to feed cattle and built fence extensions on top
of snowed-over fences to keep my cattle in.
Thousands of head of cattle were lost
from walking out on drifts and freezing
in the bitter cold winds.
When spring came, I carved out
a snowed-in yard in front of my one lone barn
so I could calf cows out,
protected from the continuing spring blizzards.
The high banks along the fences provided shelter.
The 20-foot-high drift along my house broke the wind
as well as the 25-foot-high drift in my shelter belt,
lifting the blowing snow above the cattle below.
I was younger and tougher and went
24-hour days saving new born calves
off the iced yards.
I would not want to do it over.
I know few would believe the conditions
we all worked in.
I was young, tired, and survived.

Flight or fight

High-strung and wild, the angus first-calfer
did not claim the calf she just birthed.
My standard treatment was penning her
and the calf up together
until maternal instinct kicks in.
Getting her into the barn turned out
to be trick enough, as she charged about
looking for escape.
Swinging a gate behind her,
I tried to corral her in a pen.
She turned around, hit the gate,
and proceeded to pound her full weight,
catching me in the squeeze.
I felt pain where she was hammering
the metal gate on my legs.
My hand held the bars,
knowing that you must keep your head calm
while waiting for her mayhem to cease.
When the moment came,
I climbed up and out
to the other side of the pen.
In a daze, I quit the scene
and headed for the house.
After a half-hour of applying
ice on the bumps,
I limped stiffly out
to deal with her again,
keeping on with the day.

Bad day at the ranch

My 14-year-old son was all by himself,
intent on moving a cow with a day-old calf
when the cow attacked him in the barnyard,
knocking him down and beating him up.
Badly injured, he somehow got away,
hiding in a nearby cattle chute.
He was conscious and talking
when I found him.
The white of his skull showed
where the scalp flap hung open,
a wound sliced by the angry mother cow's hoof.
Scared to death of the possibilities,
I tried to keep my voice steady,
telling him "Everything will be all right.
An ambulance is coming to take you
to a good doctor."
And my son said, "Sure, Dad."
He knew I did not know
that as I hovered over him,
he could see his own wound
mirrored in the reflection of my glasses,
saw how bad it was, and
tried his best to reassure me,
tried to keep me calm.

Unscheduled vacation

"There is no such thing as a wonderful wreck. That is like being in a fight that you weren't." – Bruce Roseland

Circling tight in a small pen,
the two-year-old white-faced Angus
got antsy.
She would not sort from a dozen calves,
instead dashing from this corner
then dashing to the next,
not seeing the open gate when presented.
In her excitement she launched over the gate,
the end of which I was holding,
making for the proverbial wreck
as her hooves caught the top bar,
swinging the gate,
and banging me up in the passing.
A cut across my leg, a bump
in the back of my head,
and my rotator cuff torn quite badly.
After two months living one-armed,
I was tired of the hurt;
an MRI said surgery.
Three months in a sling,
three months in P.T.,
then April again
and calving.

Repair

I have torn out, worn out my shoulder
doing the work I've done
10,000 times before.
To the side and up,
right arm extended,
each rep a little higher
until a power pump
to the ceiling, to the eternal sky,
ends in enough pain
to make me let my arm hang limp,
throbbing,
at my side.
The Rehab session must have been good;
I finish
with tears in my eyes.

Rites of life

As I was greasing a 3020 JD tractor,
I couldn't help but think,
"How still useful,
even though a good
fifty years since made."
Then I spied dried grass
and twigs of weeds
poking out from under the hood
where engine heat could ignite
on a hot summer day
– a bird's nest.
After removing the hood cover,
I dug
the nest out
a few finger-and-fistfuls
at a time.
This is what birds do
in the spring time,
trying to fill their world
with their own kind.
Seems like I have
known enough of us humans
who, while trying to do the same,
make a mess of our nests,
building in the wrong place.

Near miss

While holding an oil can in my right hand,
I grasp with my left hand the cover shield
on my baler's lower drive chain.
As I slide the oily tin back into place,
the tip of my fingers slip for an instant
inside, where the whirling chains spin.
Like a flash, I jerk my hand back
and stare at where fingers should be . . .
and still are.
I kiss the tips of my greasy, black digits
and breathe relief.

Next time

With fingers in our ears,
I and the butcher shop help
braced for the reverberation of the Bam!
as the sixth and final shot rang out.
The broken legged bull
finally died in the trailer
that brought him.
Unable to make the trip up the chute
to the processing kill floor
the decision had been made
to shoot him point blank
and then drag him inside by a chain.
But the single-shot breech-loaded .223
had proven to be too light
for a thick-skulled bull.
I should had shot him at home
with a proper gun if only I had known.

Farmer laureate at 63

Fifty years bouncing in a tractor seat,
Fifty years stepping across frozen mud yards,
Fifty years working in summer heat, winter cold
can get you:
both knees scoped
in order to clean out
the bent, broken cartilage;
one hernia repair;
one bicep tendon broken
and not repaired
(the doc said we can fix,
but we can't make you good again);
both shoulder rotator cuffs torn
and filled with bone spurs and arthritis;
and two 14-year-old stints in the heart
keeping an artery unplugged.
At 63, this earns me
the right to walk across my farmyard
with a fistful of wrenches
gripped in my callused hands
and the semis passing by
on the state highway blast their air horns
so that I'll look their way
and see them sitting in their cab,
giving me a wave.

Ritual

My son is attending university in Fargo,
around 260 miles one-way to come home.
His last class gets out at 9 o'clock
in the evening.
Not until then does he aim his car
for the Interstate, calling me
as he nears the state line.
Another three hours of driving in the dark
lies ahead. I say, "Stay awake,"
and he says, "I've got coffee.
I'm feeling fine –
not sleepy at all."
I turn the yard light on
and go to bed,
letting that yard light pull him
the rest of the way home.

Duct tape
Jane Green asked for it and Francie Davis started it, but Bruce finished it!

The fashionable man has, always, on hand
a roll of exotic leather
for patching holes
in jeans and shoe soles,
holding up in all kinds of weather,
keeping him well-put-together.
Now the girls may giggle as he walks about
wearing strips of this silvery pelt;
yet he may be in luck,
for they'll admire his pluck
and know he's a softy at heart –
his improvised wear has harmed no feather or hair –
he, of course, is clothed in fake Duck.

Facts of life for a native

The native prairie is made
a leaf of grass at a time
on a lean land
with moisture so sparse,
little leaches away –
black dirt slowly made.
Life lives here,
dies here –
doesn't leave.

Waiting

Drought sneaks up on us
one day at a time,
always there in our minds,
a dryness that covers a big, big space.
But things go in cycles.
Water, again, shall pour from the sky
and lay abundantly on the earth.
The wait stretches
the nerves.

Not enough grass

Drought is a sadness,
a watching of the slow
dying of the green.
For those of us who make
a living from the land,
each day flows into the next,
waiting to be saved
by a cloudburst, a change of weather,
a week of rain.
Instead, the south wind blows
hot through the month of May,
the month of June, the month of July,
August, September.
Only the shortening day stops the heat.
Nothing seems to bring rain.
Still, everyone's drought is his own.
What I do, as a rancher, is watch
cattle walk over pasture where nothing
is growing, not even weeds.
I see the grass disappear with each
bite they take, and I count the days
to when the culling must begin,
when calves must be sold,
when heavy-hearted decisions
must be made –
which cows stay and which go
to slaughter –
so the remaining number
will match
the limited amount
of winter's feed.

Mirage

On a 90-some-degree day
during a hot, dry summer,
a teaser line of thunderheads
rolls up on the far northwest horizon
and turns a soft shade of blue –
looks like rain may shower
this dusty earth.
And then, like the mirage it is,
the clouds lighten and fade
as the sun settles to bed,
streaking the sky orange,
leaving only a rainbow arc
above droughty earth
that hasn't seen a good rain
in months.

Snow and rain make grass

During a particularly miserable spring,
I grumbled to my rancher father about
the constant, every day mud, snow, and rain
through calving season.
We slogged about through the yards picking up newborns
out of the cold, wet muck,
fighting scours and pneumonia
in calves that were but days and weeks old –
tiring and endless work.
Responding to me with an edge in his voice,
he said he had known a perfect spring with every day warm,
without snow or rain.
The calving had gone without a hitch;
when the calves were born, they'd jump right up,
no problems.
"In fact," he said, "that year
the cattle had no health problems at all"
right up to the moment he ran them up the loading chute
in mid-June for the trip to the auction barn
because they had no grass
in the perfect snowless, rainless spring of 1976,
the year in which just about nothing grew.

Drought of '17

Temp hit 100 on June 2,
with an inch or less of rain for May and June combined.
Every tire track laid down in the pastures whitens and dies.
Plainly seen from the road is the little bit of living grass
that remains, paling now into a lighter shade of green,
showing where snow banks sat last winter.
Trailers roll down the dusty gravel
onto highways with cow/calf pairs
to newly scheduled sales in the auction barn.
First to go are the late calvers, then the no goods,
the broken mouths, then whole herd dispersals for
those who have no feed left to dry lot their cattle.
When the horizon does darken up,
the rain moves around the rim, slinking off to elsewhere.
Next week no rain in the forecast
except for a 20% chance on Tuesday.
On Sunday morning the probability is upped to 30.
This is how hope keeps floating even when, each day,
your eyes scan the far edge of the Western sky for any clouds,
and seeing none, your insides tighten.
This year will be remembered by its last two digits.

Absentee owner

I was in a sale barn, mid-summer,
normally a slow time,
although the auction was having a fair run of cows,
mostly young 3 to 6 year-old black Angus,
almost each one thin,
having lost a calf or been open,
and almost each one mean.
They all carried the same brand.
Entry door to the sale ring would open,
1 or 2 cows would scramble in.
The 2 ring men stayed behind
protective posts, shaking their rattle paddles
to move the cows around.
The cows frequently would charge at the slightest movement.
The auctioneer would sing-song a few bids and be done.
Several cow buyers on the seats took turns bidding.
Must have been 60 of the same sort of cows went through.
I felt sorry for the ring men, the yard men, and the guys
who had to deal with the herd these animals came from,
no owner to be seen sitting
watching the sale.

Montana is burning
September 13, 2017

Montana is on fire.
The Dakotas are covered in smoke.
I cannot see the horizon for all the gray draped in between.
The sun sets angry red,
after spending the day crossing
a cloudless, hazy sky,
giving us a hundred degree September heat.
Doomsday hangs under this shroud,
coming from flames out of control
that thousands of men are trying to contain
far off to the Northwest.
No mercy there.
I am breathing the death of a million trees.

Defiance

Wave after wave of Great Canadas
interspersed with groupings
of white snow geese
fill the arc of autumn sky
above golden Dakota fields.
Weeks earlier, they must have lifted off
from the waters of the Northland,
their ancient migration trails
crossing southward over a landscape
increasingly tamed into farmland.
These descendants of the ancient migrations
soar through black air,
their honking a chorus of voices
that carries for miles,
claiming this air, this earth,
as their domain,
finding what they need,
making another passage
in the year of our Lord, 2012.

Getting ahead of the forecast

For months, only hawks and eagles made solitary flights
over nearly-bare snow-covered prairie,
snatching unwary pheasants
and rabbits who stirred.
Only clouds and these large-bird predators
owned the winter sky,
until March
when the first flight of geese appear, long necks outstretched,
black and white against gray sky, honking northbound.
"Now," I say to myself, "spring is here."
Within the week, however, I look up to see geese
winging southward.
What do they know?
A day later,
the wind turns raw; snow falls –
not quite the end of winter and perhaps not yet spring.
The geese, like me, were premature in their optimism.

Night moves

Around midnight
each and every early spring,
you would think
all good husbands and wives
should be snug in bed.
Instead, cowmen and cowwomen
are on the move making cow checks,
seeing if 1st-calf heifers
are off in the far dark corners,
knee deep in muddy pens,
restless, sniffing the ground
and swishing their tails.
Always seems like a big, low pressure threatens
with the weatherman saying blizzard;
a foot of snow and high wind.
Beware!
If only both of you had known
when the " I do " vows were being said
the next words should have been:
"You'll be first –
except when it comes to calving"
then the cow babies just about always win.
Husbands and wives do their bonding
at this time of year
as they grip hands tenderly, firmly,
bringing wet, slippery, new bovine life in.

The primeval heart
April 2013

Whipped by blizzardly wind,
pellets of sleet and snow
sting my skin like fire.
I could not set my face
into this wind.
Instead, with head bowed
and half-blinded,
I make trip after trip
back into the herd
to pull one after another
half-frozen, covered-in-muck
newborn calf to the inside shelter
of the barn.
Some of the calves' mothers would follow
some would not,
driven half mad
by birthing a calf into a whited-out world
of wet cold

and howling wind that holds no mercy.
Those who would not follow
would have to be paired up later,
after their babies were warmed up,
dried off . . . when time would permit.
Meanwhile the work of cutting losses,
saving the strong, making do had to go on
until the storm abated.
Looking out from the barn door
into fury
so much bigger,
so much stronger than myself,
the thought of letting go, giving up,
letting the gods of storm
take all away pulsed in my fears.
But how can you quit
when each small calf that you carry inside
to lay on the straw
has a heart that beats
with a will to survive,
a will that is the same
that beats in my own heart,
primeval.

First calf

Due date was getting near.
I was checking the first-calf heifers
that had been yarded separately from the main herd.
I could see some of them, young Angus,
huddled together near the fence,
heads pointed in, obviously interested in something.
On some days, that might have been just a cat,
but on this fine, early-spring day, as I drew near
I could see that the something was a good-sized
baby calf, head up, alert,
legs folded under like they were supposed to be.
He was unconcerned with the attention that all these
soon-to-be-first-time mothers
were bestowing upon him.
His own mother was not hard to pick out – she was the one
who was keeping a constant eye on him
as she moved about, occasionally sniffing her baby
and then giving forth a short beller.

I went back and got my small tractor
with hitch-mounted calf-carrier attached,
in order to cart the newborn up closer
to the buildings for shelter and to get him away
from the curious crowd of first-calf heifers.
As I picked the calf up,
I got whacked in the face by the newborn's wet nose.
He flopped around, letting me know
he had his own terms with the world.
The new mother followed well,
along with a bunch of the other two-year-olds –
a parade of sorts.
They were excited to have something new.
I placed the mother and calf
in a separate yard so they could get more
familiar with each other, a promising beginning.
The remaining curious two-year-olds,
as they were turned away by the gate,
ran back to join the others,
their own time soon to come.

Calving season

A time of the year
when my world makes total sense
is calving,
new life born in straw, dirt,
and birthing fluids:
the stuff of life,
a time when the choice is made
to fight for life,
no "To be or not to be."
From the first gasp of air
into the newborn's lungs,
that question is settled.

The will to survive

The calf was birthed into cold, wet mud
with the temperature barely in the upper thirties.
A light, spring rain was keeping conditions miserable and slick.
The calf, with spindly, unsteady legs, was trying to get up,
flopping first to one side and then to the other.
His back legs would get footing,
but then his front feet would slip in the wetness
and down he would tumble into the gunk,
making himself into a matted mud ball.
His mother, standing less than five feet away,
watched anxiously,
occasionally giving him a nudge and a lick,
claiming him – his struggle was her struggle,
his fate was her concern.
After each attempt, the calf kept his head up and rested,
then lurched forward again, trying to get his legs extended.
I have seen this process many times,
seen which are the strong, which are the determined,
and which ones will need my assistance.
If they make it upright and to the udder,
they will live.
This one was not showing any sign of quitting.
This one would get up on his own.
And he did.

Easter morning 2015

New calf standing, trembling upright
in dawn's first light,
blue sky above,
northeast wind blowing,
a hint of rain in the air.
New calf's eyes opening wide,
nose to nose with mom
who is staring back
just as big eyed.

Hidden in plain sight

Even after this particularly wet spring,
an indifferent eye would likely not see
the acres and acres of mayflowers
that make the wild prairie hillsides
their garden plots.
Less than six inches tall,
the pale blue pasques
are so short
they scarcely wave in the breeze.
Instead, they stay nearly hidden
among the stems of last year's grasses.
Like much else in this land,
usually only the practiced eye of the native
sees the beauty in the background
others see as plain.

Slap!

Such a short time between
loving what spring has brought
and mosquitoes.

Last calf

Nearing dark, my cousin's last cow to calf,
a black Angus three-year-old,
was having trouble delivering.
We had her caught standing upright
in an outside headgate.
I found that the calf's head
was pushed to the side and back.
With much effort
I straightened the head,
got the front legs straight through the pelvis,
and double-hitched each leg properly
with the calving chains,
all the while the calf inside the cow
would give a twitch,
signaling, "I'm alive – get me out."
With a steady pull
a big bull calf, eyes wide open,
was soon lying on the ground,
wet in his mother's blood
and his own birthing fluids.
By then, my shirt was soaked,
both with the efforts of delivering the calf
and with the dampness of a summer rain.

Compulsion

Every rancher has a date
to turn out bulls,
practically a religion,
a day we can't skip.
Mine is June 20th.
This year it rained the night before
and most of all day of the 20th.
Late in the afternoon,
the weather backed off some,
giving me a chance to get the bulls in
and run them into my stock-trailer
then head down the section-line dirt road
which has turned to mud and puddles.
Rain started falling again from the sky.
Promptly, I slid off the road track into soft ground –
stuck.
My help pulled me out with a front-wheel-assist tractor.
I took another run down the rutted lane,
almost making the top of a hill,
got stuck again.

Tractor came along and pulled me out.
Over and over
we did this routine
until we got
to the cow pasture
and turned boys with girls.
With a lighter load,
I nearly made the return trip
before getting stuck again, short of home.
Tractor drove up, pulled me out.
By now it was nearly dark,
rain still falling.
Next morning: three additional inches
in the rain gauge
with water standing or running everywhere.

A cow's gestation period is a bit more
than nine months.
Most likely there will be yet
snow on the ground
when I'll get my first live calf,
conceived on a summer day
of big rain.

The gift bearer

Across hundreds of miles
of upper Midwest plains,
wisps of warm moisture
in the form of cumulus clouds
are pulled in circular motion
above rolling, checker-boarded crop
and prairie land.
Northeast by southwest, the sweep
of puffy clouds rolls around and around,
pulled by the low/high pressures
of nature's weather pumps,
priming the warm, wet air to butt up against
the Canadian cold front.
Clouds pile and push higher and higher —
an elevator ride
that turns vapor into a storm
of thunderheads:
wind scream
rain pound
hail pelt
lightning flash.
Wind/rain/ice/and fire,
the destroyer/the giver
of life.

None of my business

While driving down a black-top road,
I see a large group
of yearling replacement heifers
in a pasture without a bull.
They're rushing up to a cross-fence
to greet a couple of the neighbor's big bulls
standing on the other side
of three rusty wires.
The two different neighbors
have a long history of not getting along.
They own these separate but adjoining pastures.
I'm sure turn-out time for either side
is at least 10 days away.
"Gee," I wonder as I continue on my way,
"how will this unfold?"

Bull-headed

One of my Black Angus bulls
has had enough of heat, flies,
and fellow cattle company,
so he walks into a slough of water
until chest deep, and there he stays,
even though I drive the rest of the herd
to another pasture. He gets left behind.
In the weeks that follow, whenever the day is hot
he stands neck deep in the water.
In the cool of the morning and the evening,
he eats grass on the hillside, sits and rests.
But whenever I come near,
he walks back into the slough
and stands there, soaking in deep water,
knowing I can't follow –
a stubborn game both of us play.
The advantage seems on his side
until five 12-guage shotgun blasts
in front of his nose
persuade him to swim out.
Effective communication is the key
to solving stand-offs.

Day's end

In the west,
a thundercloud
peeks over the horizon,
a tip-off to tomorrow
as darkness grows blacker
on a short June night –
only a few hours of sleep
until the summer work continues.

The drawback

In my darkened room at bedtime,
the bright light of the full moon
comes through my window,
not a cloud in the night sky
to dim the glow.
After a hard day,
it's all I can do to keep from hollering,
"Will someone tell that moon
to shut off the lights?"

Work buddies

Perched motionless
on the top wire of a barbed-wire fence
in 90-degree, windless heat
are dragonflies
clinging to the razor-sharp tips of the barbs.
Some are golden-colored; some have clear wings
that are black-striped; others are bright neon blue.
When I come near, they spring upward,
hovering in a blur of wings,
soon to seek yet another sharp-edged barb
of the new fence on which I am
clipping wire after wire
to the steel "T" posts.

The haymaker's dance

In July's 90 degree humid heat,
three days after a heavy rain,
I'm trying to bale hay left
laid down flat, unraked.
Water and mud lie in low spots,
which I must either drive around –
thus leaving the hay to rot,
or drive through – mixing the wet in with the dry,
salvaging what I can.
Although frustrated with the work, I make progress
thanks to sunshine and some breeze.
After several hours, I smell a faint whiff of smoke –
I stop several times and walk around
the tractor and the baler.
Everything seems to check out.
Then I clean the chaff off the chains
and there, plain to see, is a bearing gone bad.
No more baling for today.
Tomorrow, I'll have to head to town for repairs.
The one-step-forward has turned into one-step-back.

The best-laid web

The silky, white oval of the spider-web
looked perfectly woven atop the windrow of hay –
a good day's work of spinning
by a spider hidden
somewhere below the spiral
leading to his lair.
He would be waiting
for a juicy insect to get ensnared
and start yanking on the web strands.
But I was raking,
turning over the windrow to dry,
rolling the spider-web along with the hay;
then later, in the heat of the day,
baling up the hay, spider-web and all.
And if the spider hung around,
he, too, would be rolled up inside the bale
and there he would be stuck.
"That's tough," I thought.
"That's tough."

The other side

On the other side of the windowpane
is the dark of summer's night.
Moths, one by one, frantically beat
their wings against the glass,
trying to get to the light
on the other side.
I sit and watch in my easy chair
as, one by one, they drop to the wet grass
outside,
exhausted.

Man vs plants

In the hot humid days of August,
corn that was not knee high
by the cooler-than-average Fourth of July,
has now jumped, making 8-foot-tall, tasseled forests.
So too have the weeds
in all places not sprayed or mowed.
The wire gates I had carelessly dropped
onto the ground alongside my fences,
plus my misplaced work tools,
I now struggle to find,
hidden in a profusion of green growth.
What once was left lying
on the nearly bare ground of May,
I must now rip from the grasp
of entwining grass, vines,
and towering sunflowers,
whose yellow-petaled heads snap off,
casualties of an ongoing war
as I free my stuff from the vegetative god
that I so welcomed just a few months ago.

August/cow country

In August, when the ripened
grass seed heads cast
a golden white glaze across pasture lands,
black cows, bellies filled
from their morning graze,
walk into the breeze,
fan out, spread across
the rolling land, swing their tails
at rising flies
stirred by noonday heat.
The cows' calves follow a length or two behind,
smaller steps trailing
their mothers' longer strides.
The days of summer fill,
move forward
what the early April snows of spring began.

Good day's work

New wood touches new wood,
straight lines of matching boards
laid alongside, one after another,
and lag-screwed into the rubber sides
of a ten-foot-wide tire tank.
The excess is trimmed off with an electric saw,
making a good, tight cover
for a cattle watering tank.
Hard work, but good work to do
when the sun is blazing hot
and the sweat soaks my shirt.
Heat from the sun goes all the way
into my shoulder bones.
Come winter, cattle will drink
from the tank's open end,
water kept warm by artesian flow
and the float not frozen in
from the 20-below winter wind –
all because of work done
on this sunny August day.

Inheritance

It's 10:30 in the morning.
I'm still at the kitchen table
doing mundane paperwork,
paying bills,
working on my second pot of coffee.
There's work to be done outside,
machinery to be fixed, and
all the other tasks
of keeping a ranch running.
I keep hearing the voice
of my father who would be having fits
that I was still in the house
so late in the morning.
Unless you were outside,
no real work was getting done.
I, at age 61, still hear his voice, insisting,
"What's the holdup?!"

Late October

Red-on-black box elder bugs fly,
bouncing sideways off the sunny side of the house
and scamper to the nearest foundation crack.
Pesky flies crawl about, rotating east to west
from one outside windowpane to the next
as sunlight arches overhead.
Cold is coming.
The bugs and I both know it:
a night of killing frost soon.
Three seasons completed – spring, summer, fall.
I feel gratitude for making it through a season of work again.
Not until January will I think of the cold, silent air
as too quiet and too thin.

Weed seed celebration

Nearing the 1st of November,
tall weeds in pastures, ditches, and lots
are brittle and whitened, their juices dried up
by killing frosts.
Their seed heads hang heavy, ready to shatter
like confetti, ready to fly willy-nilly through the air,
piling thickly on the hood and windshield
of my pickup whenever I travel off road
through these pastures and fields –
my own, private ticker-tape parade.

Miserable
or a state of mind

My help and I stand in cold rain,
shoulders hunched, working reluctant cattle,
sorting them in the corrals,
poking and pushing them down the chute,
sliding in mud-weighted-down boots,
clothes clinging to chilled skin –
miserable, monotonous, dangerous work.
All you can do is keep going,
knowing that no one is happy
with you for having picked this day,
and you're more than a little mad
at the weatherman's "80% partly cloudy"
dripping off the brim of your hat.

The promise

After Thanksgiving, the grass is dead,
brown but for the last tint of green near its roots;
below that, an inch-and-one-half of frost in the ground
which requires wiggling my spade a bit
to make a starter hole
for a gate post. With that done,
my tractor-mounted post-hole auger
bites in, spinning dirt out easily
a full four feet down,
mounding dirt into a circle.
I lift an eight-foot railroad tie
straight up to a grey, chilled sky,
then let it drop into the 12-inch wide hole.
Kneeling down, I squeeze freshly dug loose soil.
Feels wet.
Next spring the grass will be green.
Kicking dirt in,
I set the post and tamp steadily.

Fall weaning

For three days and three nights
they stand at the gate
where they have last seen their calves.
Full-throated in their bawling, they call
for their calves to relieve their swollen udders,
their voices going raspy,
eyes glazing from the repetition
never answered.
On the fourth day, hope gives out,
with only a few pacing to the gate
to wail of their longing.

Cull cows

Sorted out, left behind
as the rest of your herdmates
go out the gate,
for you there's a different fate
than the daily routine of waiting
for the feeding tractor to show up,
lazing around through the winter
as your calf inside gestates,
blooming like the spring flowers will bloom.
Coming up open at preg-testing
makes for an entirely different story.
A cowman's eye is a sad eye but a hard eye
when the vet says, "Open."

Poet as full-time cowman

If you think a pen
and a few words
are a mighty thing,
try fixing a broken feeder wagon's
cross chain with your choicest cuss words
on a cold day in a tractor
as you drive away from cattle
only half-fed, looking puzzled.

Gimme shelter

The wind hurls and spits snow
in blinding gusts that sting exposed skin
with a below-zero bite.
While sitting in the fortress of my tractor cab,
fan blowing heated air full-on,
tires bouncing on frozen ground,
I feed bales to a herd of black Angus,
their backs white with snow.
The cows huddle together,
trying to hide from the arctic cold.
They are so miserable
only the most hungry eat the hay I dump.
Jackrabbits that have crept in from the storm
are startled by the movement of my tractor.
They run out into the swirling snow
of the blizzard only to return,
crouching low to the ground,
choosing the scant shelter of the cattle
over flight.

Eden retold

In the winter, summer gestates.
The foolish may think all hope of life lies defeated
in this cold, silent land
never to be born, a closed grave where despair dwells.
So much of what is seen appears to be barren.
But time brings truth –
winter is but a long sleep,
and inside the sleep is the seed –
hope enough until the world
becomes another spring.

Fattening up

Eight inches of snow on the level,
temperatures not much above freezing.
A light northwest wind blowing;
cloudy, but the recent storm has moved off.
Black cull cows are seen out my house window
eating at their feed bunks,
trailing one by one to the water tank
and back to feed, getting fuller and full,
just waiting to be sold.
The white snow, like Christmas,
wrapping my view.

The belly of a cow

It is through the belly of a cow
that I find the means to pay my bills
and buy my meals.
It is through the belly of a cow
I feed the grass that I mowed and stacked
all summer long.
The belly of a cow cares not
if I am happy or sad,
cold or hot, if it is raining
or the sun is shining.
It only cares that it gets fed,
regular like,
that it is satisfied.

Buy a cow and save the planet

When I hear about the back-to-nature-folks,
the ones who save their kitchen scraps
and pile them up back of their suburban houses
in order to give their gardens a little organic kick,
I also get to thinking about those
who make their living from cows
and spend many a day following behind them,
stepping in the aftermath of what cows do.
After ingesting veggies from morning to night,
a cow chews it once, then, as a cud,
chews it twice, swallowing
and fermenting its veggie stew
through four stomachs, and then returns it
out the back for nature to reuse.
That's what cowboys think a good composter should do.
So if you wish to save the planet
and keep your carbon footprint small,
get some cows,
raise yourself up at 6 every morning,
pull on your cowhide boots,
saddle up your 4-wheeler, horse, or truck
and ride for the Bovine Mobile Composter brand.
Save the green Earth
one cow pie at a time.

Moonshine

There is always something mystical
about a sky lighted by moonshine.
Stars are present,
but gentler;
clouds floating
across the night sky are a translucent white.
The moonlit earth
can be traveled about
without need of any additional light.
I have stood in the middle of my yard
and read a newspaper by moonshine.
When was it that we became afraid
of the dark, like death,
hiding in our cities of light?
In doing so we lost
that half of the night
that is moonshine.
With the full moon upon the countryside,
it's easy to imagine
walking out, striding over the land,
disappearing into the shadows to find
the mystery that you know has
always been on the very edge of your life.
Find a road.
Follow the moonshine.

Rock of ages

Outside, around the corner of my house,
lies a rock that was hauled
from a field I was clearing.
This one I could not cast off into a
jumbled rock pile to be buried.
No, this one I had to save,
having driven by it countless times
while checking pasture fence.
I marveled at its 2-to-4-inch-wide veins
of pinkish white criss-crossing the deep grey
granite that weighed a ton.
Veins bulged out
from the rock's surface,
looking like cryptic runes,
seemingly messages to the world
pressed into eternal rock,
asking to be deciphered,
asking since being birthed from a mountain
by a glacier and then set down
thousands of years ago,

asking midnight stars, thunderstorms and snows,
asking wolves and buffalo,
asking prairie flowers and waving grasses,
asking all the way back to an unknown past.
My wife insists that it shall
come to rest upon my grave
if she has any say.
For now, I keep the weeds and tall grass neat
around this heavy rock
while puzzling over what it would say,
if only it could.
If this rock does become my marker,
not many can say they tended the stone
that sits on their grave.
But please, do not engrave or deface the rock veins
that tried so hard to speak to me.
Alongside, just put a plate that has written on it,
"Here lies Bruce. Sit awhile and rest your feet."

Real estate open house

The wild mallards of fall, the ones we see flying in flocks,
whistling overhead in the grey-laden autumn sky,
are different upon their return in the spring,
no longer wary and watchful of humans.
I see these ducks going about their business,
waddling out of the snow-melt ponds two-by-two,
hen and drake,
walking on the short, greening grass with their webbed feet –
seemingly with no set direction in mind – madly in love,
unhurried, paying no more mind to me
than they would to a fence post
or to the cows I'm caring for in the calving pastures.
These contented ducks, at their slow, slow pace,
know what they are doing,
checking out the neighborhood, seeing if this pond,
this pasture, is a good place to settle in
and raise a family.

Ablution

In my backyard garden,
a rooster pheasant in turquoise plumage
crouches in a shallow dip of ground,
his clawed, spurred feet scratching,
kicking dry dirt into his ruffled feathers.
Sideways his long neck arches
back and forth,
his beak pecking, flicking grit
into the air for a head
to tail dirt bath.

All is not over

The fall freezes have blighted
my backyard garden.
The tomato vines are limp, pale green ropes;
the cantaloupe and squash hills are stricken,
the leaves yellowing to brown, crumpled edges;
the radish row is an empty memory.
All that remains is sickly,
except for carrots,
their green, leafy tops
immune yet to frosty nights.
I push my spade in deep,
next to this long-season crop,
pulling back, heaving black dirt
and bright orange carrots to sunlight,
carrots so crisp they crack in two with but a touch.
They are so sweet – the last fresh garden treat.
I gather them up in my arms,
trim the tops off, and clean them up.
In my mind, I already have one foot
into the next spring.

Mates

Staying close,
they hunt as a pair,
these two red foxes
whose pawprints crisscross
through my farmyards.
I see them as they hunt,
early morning and in the gathering twilight,
two orangish-red streaks of flame,
following their noses, snuffling scents,
shopping for tidbits that make up their meals.
Their ears are constant perked-up triangles
of alertness, listening for the scratching
of a mouse stirring in dry grass.
So focused are these foxes
for the signs of hidden prey
that they do not notice me
anymore than they would notice
a cow or a tree.
Since they are not the hunted,
only in my movement do they see me.
Then, with a whip of their long, red tails,
they race for the taller weeds.

Night hunter

As dusk greys down, a great horned owl,
with a few flaps of his wings,
sails tree-top level overhead
from one shelter belt to another.
During the day, he was but a silent clump
hidden high in a crotch of some branch;
but now, with the western sun a red,
diminishing glare,
he is all ears and feathers and talons.

His meal

Twenty years of mix-matched
black, white and orange cats
have given rise to the calico cat
that claims rights on my farm.
The cats here are not pets, but hunters,
always keeping a wary eye on my doings
and slipping away whenever I draw too near.
On Christmas Day evening
as I approach my house,
the farm's resident calico cat
jumps out of the cat-food pan
I had just filled that very morning
and pauses next to the cement foundation
and waits in the half-light
for his world to be quitted of me.
I walk through the house door,
leaving him to his domain.

Momma cat

The mother cat hunts herself thin,
bringing mice and rabbits in
to feed her fat baby furballs
hidden in the lilac bushes next to our house.
Her only rest is when she stretches out to nurse
her grey and orange-striped litter;
she holds her head up,
eyes half-closed, watchful, yet soft,
as the kittens knead her softly with their paws.

Taking a walk on the wild side

After a quick January thaw,
a smeared paw print lies frozen
in the mud alongside my machine shed,
showing a fox in a hurry.
Months will pass before spring rain
will soften the paw print,
smoothing it
to the point of being again just mud,
no longer a reminder of my surprise
at seeing a clue
to the wild coming out
and taking a walk on a warm
winter night
while I slept.

Sanctuary

Two red foxes, mates,
each nearly the same size
and having a black spot on each hindquarter,
have set up a den on my farmstead.
Their kits, small, shy things,
reddish and smoky grey,
are being reared just fifty yards from my house,
peeking in and out of their burrow
that's in and under an old bale stack.
Frequently one of the adults will sit lookout
atop an old, weathered bale,
cautiously watching me as I go about
my everyday routine.
The mates are constantly hunting,
loping along with noses to the ground.
When I see them,
sunrises and sunsets,
they barely notice me
and if they do,

they act like they just remembered
they shouldn't trust me,
even though I am one of the few
that will not shoot them.
They get some pheasants,
of which I have too many,
and they thin out the mice and rabbits,
which I will not miss.
The spring-calving cattle in the yards
pay them little heed
since each is not much bigger
than a large tomcat.
Sooner or later, they will go into the bigger world
and perhaps someone
will sight a bead on them.
But until then,
they run free.

Night begins

Silhouetted against the deep red sunset,
the great horned owl flaps his wings,
launching himself into the biting early-March air.
With silent, yellow eyes blinking,
the great bird had waited,
talons grasping the bending branches
of an ash tree,
all day of a late winter.
A cold front had passed through
with 40-mile-an-hour sweeps of snow.
With dusk, the winds had quieted.
Now with the near-silent swoosh of feathers,
this night's prowl begins,
hunting the scratchy trails
of mice racing across icy snow.

Return of the native

Antelope – two babies, two moms, one buck
and four yearlings – shouldn't have been there
grazing in my newly-cut alfalfa field,
but there they were – 140 years after their kind had been
run off, shot out, erased from my land
just like the buffalo.
Their heads jerked up and off they were,
making dust, staying in a compact bunch,
their small, fat rumps flashing white as they
turned deftly through a fence gate,
gathering speed as they sprinted halfway across
the next field.
Then, thinking better of their direction, they
made a 45-degree turn in their flight,
headed out the nearest section-line gate,
and proceeded north and out of my sight.
They knew the lay of the land
as well as I did.

Good earth

On the first day of an early spring,
the ground has thawed
and I am in my small plot of garden,
stepping on a long-handled shovel,
turning over the earth.
At 60 years of age, my knees creak
and twinge with wear.
I think of my Norwegian, Irish, German
and French ancestors,
all tillers of soil, hands calloused,
gripping the well-worn handles of their
shovels and hoes.
With each seed they sowed
by the sweat of their labor,
they earned their tomorrow;
from an Old World to a New World,
they made a harvest of dreams
by the simple, steadfast act
of turning over the earth,
just as I now turn over mine,
making a seedbed,
smelling the rawness
that freshly-turned earth exhales –
the promise of new life
springing from an awakening ground.
I have learned the art and craft
of growing food –
such work that a lifetime can go by
with not a day spent in regret.
The day approaches
when I shall lie down with them.
We have made good company
for each other.

Net worth

What is the asking price
for the land I stand on,
the tools, machines, nuts and bolts,
that can go for bid?
The house I lived in
could be jacked up and carted away.
My cows are readily financially convertible,
truckable, sellable.
Just like that – sold.
All that can be touched is an asset,
a dollar amount, a potential bank account.
But when I lean on my barbed-wire fence
and look across the landscape,
whether on a bitter, short day
when the wind blows 20 MPH
at 20 degrees below
while I watch the snow constantly shift,
or in mid-June
when the sun rises early and sets late
and the grass is green
and all the birds, bugs, and beasts
are driven to procreate.
Either way, on good days
or on some of the worst,
as I pause to let the scene sink in,
only then do I feel rich.

Hot-tubbing on New Year's Eve

During a three-day blizzard, a half-grown heifer calf,
around six-hundred pounds, slid her entire body
into a big-tire water tank on my farm,
a tight fit; she was unable to scramble out.
She stood hot-tubbing in artesian water that was 70 degrees,
no doubt feeling better than being blasted
by the 35-below wind-chilled air.
I saw the near-frozen calf, bottom half submerged,
top half iced-over, rear-end to my view,
in the dying light of this year's last day.
When I grabbed her tail and gave a hard pull,
the 600-lb. calfcicle let me know with a kick she was still alive.
With a 20-ft. chain I always carry in my tractor,
I dipped my arms past the elbows into the tank,
wrapped the chain around the Angus's thigh,
and then hooked the other end of chain around my tractor's
hitch.
A little of my frostbitten skin
stuck to the chain links.
After I climbed into my tractor cab. I couldn't see a thing;
all the windows were frosted-over white.
The choice was simple: leave the calf to die of exposure
or give a yank – maybe break a leg –
or even drown the calf in the process.
I rolled the tractor ahead about a dozen feet.
In the 40-plus MPH wind,
I opened the cab to see how the mess had gone.
Lo and behold, an icicled and dripping-wet 600-lb. heifer
scrambled on by in a dead run to join her herdmates
back at the tree windbreak.

A year turns

I arise early, as usual, for chores on this first day of the New Year;
new or old, cattle pay no heed but to their stomachs.
Making sure these cattle are satisfied
has given order to my years and days.
As dawn comes, a stiff wind ripples
the field-brown prairie grasses
in waves lapping to the horizon.
The sky above is pale winter blue,
a winter of almost no snow so far.
I carry one bale after another
out the gate to be dropped
and then surrounded by cattle
nuzzling in, seeking the choicest leaves.
The land, caught in wintry sleep,
has the look of a well-worn work glove.
I know every dip, turn, and wrinkle
stretching outward from me,
ciphers that I continue to try to read.
When the feeding is done,
I take a moment to sit quietly as my cab
is rocked slightly back and forth
by a gusty wind.
I watch this New Year unfold across a horizon that is miles wide
and thousands of years in the making
under a sky that goes into infinity.
On such a day as this,
I can hear the land talking,
moving along from the past
and into the future.

Where the heart is

Give me the open sky
where my sky is my lake.
There I'll swim from
morning to night.
Give me the waving grass,
as though the grass were waves
on a sea,
and let the cattle I raise
be like sailing ships
coming to dock in a good bay.
Let me give thanks
for living where my heart is.

A regular

You'll find me where light meets darkness,
where earth touches sky.
Like a songbird's trill at dawn,
I am here only for a little while.
But as long as I am able,
I shall greet each new day
in my open-air cathedral,
saying my daily grace
with early morning sunshine
full upon my thankful face.

About the author

Bruce Roseland's first book, *The Last Buffalo*, published in 2006, won the 2007 Wrangler Award for Outstanding Book of Poetry by the National Cowboy and Western Heritage Museum. The sequel to that book, *A Prairie Prayer*, published in 2008, won the 2009 Will Rogers Medallion Award. In the spring of 2012, Roseland published a third book of poems entitled *Church of the Holy Sunrise*, a volume that contains correlating photos by Susan Melius. In the spring of 2014, Scurfpea published his book *Song For my Mother*. Roseland's book *Gift of Moments*, with artwork by Doris Symens Armstrong, was published by Scurfpea in 2016.

Cowman and other books written by Bruce are available at *amazon.com* and many local bookstores.

www.ingramcontent.com/pod-product-compliance
Lightning Source LLC
Chambersburg PA
CBHW032053150426
43194CB00006B/516